PLASTIC JEWELRY

Lyngerda Kelley
Nancy Schiffer

West Chester, Pennsylvania 19380

Black Bakelite and brass pin. Red Bakelite bracelet in shape of face. Red Bakelite and brass pin jointed bracelet. Gold colored plastic hair ornament. Silver and red Bakelite earrings. (Bizarre Bazaar)

Printed in the United States of America.
ISBN: 0-88740-109-0
Published by Schiffer Publishing Ltd.
1469 Morstein Road, West Chester, Pennsylvania 19380

This book may be purchased from the publisher. Please include $2.00 postage. Try your bookstore first.

Contents

Acknowledgments

The fun and novelty of wearing, collecting or studying plastic jewelry easily becomes contagious. There is no end to design, style, color or innovation. In our efforts to explore collectable plastic jewelry many people provided their ideas, sources, skills, as well as their collections, as the world of plastic jewelry rapidly grew. We are grateful to Marian R. Carroll, Dennis Cogdell, Frances Cronan and Frances Detweiler, Jackie Fleischmann, and Aggie Moore at the Black Angus Antique Mall, Adamstown, PA; Ann's Arts in Chestnut Hill, PA; Maureen McEvoy and Linda Morgan at the Islington Antique Mall, London; Rebecca Frey, Joan Leibowitz, and Lorraine Matt at The Lafayette Mill Antique Center, Lafayette, N.J.; Nora Lee at Bizarre Bazaar and Terry Rogers at The Manhattan Art and Antique Center, N.Y.C.; Bob Coyle and Marianne Ward at The People's Store, Lambertville, N.J., Mim Klein in Philadelphia; Miss Genevieve and Kenneth J. Lane of Kenneth J. Lane, Inc., Patricia Funt, Michael Greenberg, Muriel Karasik, Angela Kramer, Carol Lupo at Trifari, Mark and Malvina Solomon and Fred Baekeland, N.Y. City; Ann Seeger and Robert Harding of the Smithsonian Institution, Washington, D.C.; Howard Aurbach and Ken Mafia of As Time Goes By in New Hope, P.A.; Karen Carmichael, Henry Chitwood, Wanda Johnson, Matilda D. Knowles II, Judy Pyle, Neal Davis, and Scott and Wendy Tyson.

Evolution of Plastic Jewelry

Colorful, lightweight and formerly inexpensive, plastic jewelry has been taken for granted in the past. But plastics have come of age. Now they are sought after as collectibles of skyrocketing value.

Bakelite, Lucite, and celluloid have become distinct names representing easily differentiated synthetic plastics found in jewelry over the last hundred years. The moldable property of plastics enabled this jewelry to be mass produced and originally inexpensive, yet of unique designs with many variations. Although molded, a great deal of hand-operated decoration has resulted in few identical pieces.

Many examples of colorful jewelry made from natural and synthetic plastics are presented in the following pages. The materials are explained, and a brief history of the styles will enable collectors to estimate dates of manufacture more readily. The manufacturers of plastic jewelry are for the most part unknown, since almost none of this jewelry was marked in any way until the most recent time.

The word "Plastic" comes from the Greek *Plastikos:* to mold or form. Plastic can be defined broadly as an inherently formless material which can be shaped under heat and pressure.

Molded black gutta percha pin, early example. (Jackie Fleischmann)

Plastic materials are divided into two groups, natural and synthetic. Natural plastics include amber, horn, tortoiseshell, and insect secretions that are used to make shellac. Gutta percha and rubber in its simplest form are conditions. Cellulose, Bakelite, casein, and Lucite are among the synthetic from chemical reactions which take place under carefully controlled conditions. Cellulose, bakelite, casein, and lucite are among the synthetic plastics. Today the term "plastic" in its popular usage is taken to mean a synthetic material.

Jewelry has been made from natural plastics since ancient times. Amber, ivory and tortoiseshell have been shaped into beads for necklaces and used alone for bracelets, pins and hair ornaments, especially in the late nineteenth century.

In the second half of the nineteenth century, many scientific discoveries and industrial mechanization forever changed the products we use and our way of life. Advances in chemistry brought about the invention of cellulose plastic in 1867, casein plastic in 1897, and Bakelite resin plastic in 1907. These materials all were molded into countless useful products including jewelry.

In the early 1920's, when cast synthetic resins were found to be easy to work and color, jewelry manufacturers began experimenting with the new material to produce beads, molded pins and bangle bracelets. Wood, butterflies, and other materials were found able to be imbedded unharmed when the resin was cast around them. Mottled effects and pearlized finishes were gradually controlled in the 1920's. Therefore, inexpensive imitations of pearls were mass-produced from that time.

Bakelite trademark from 1939 Worlds Fair. Molded on H-P-M. Injection machine made by the Hydraulic Press Mfg. Co. Bakelite trademark registered U.S. Patent Office. (Karen Carmichael)

Synthetic plastics were highly successful in imitating the natural plastics like amber, horn, ivory, and tortoiseshell and continued to do so for many years. In 1919, celluloid jewelry was imported from Paris in a vast array of colors such as French blue, mottled green, yellow, white, purple and shell. These were made into pendants and ornaments strung on ribbon or as the links themselves. Galalith (a celluloid) was most popular in 1921 when it was frequently cut into different shapes or combined with metal for pins and necklaces. Then, with new designs of short sleeved gowns, bracelets were worn in profusion. Frequently both Bakelite and Galalith were set with rhinestones.

In the beginning, novelty plastic jewelry was purchased primarily by women looking for inexpensive colorful jewelry. However, it gained more universal appeal after 1925 when French clothing designer Co-Co Chanel introduced the idea of costume jewelry in her couture collections. Chanel also designed real jewelry which was often copied in plastic and other materials. It was not until the late 1930's that fashion magazines would recognize costume jewelry and even then there was very little discussion of plastic jewelry.

The Art Deco period, about 1925-1930 provided a boon to plastic jewelry with its geometrics, zigzag patterns and sleek style influences. Some French designers experimented with plastic, then, however they seldom signed their pieces. The workmanship found in plastic jewelry of this time is very good.

One person to know great success in the production of plastic jewelry in the 1920's in America was George F. Berkander. His company was located in Providence, Rhode Island which was, and is, one of the country's centers for the production of costume and novelty jewelry. Berkander began producing tortoise shell hair combs. In observing the rapidly changing styles in women's fashions, he progressed to bar pins which he eventually set with pearls and rhinestones and even some gold plated design elements.

Red Bakelite "Victory" pin with banner, c. 1940. (Wendy Tyson)

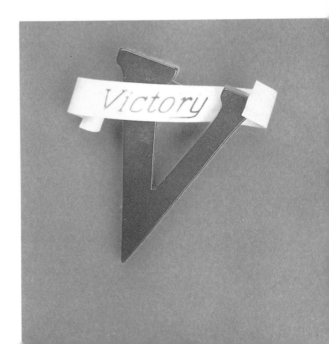

All of this he accomplished using plastic as his medium. By 1931 Berkander was making inexpensive bracelets at better than a thousand gross daily, using three tons of plastic materials a day. Berkander took credit for developing the first cellulose acitate flower pins, "celluloid elephant chains for the wives of Presidents Harding and Coolidge; and tiny celluloid airplanes with Lingbergh's name on them were ready for sale when the flyer landed in Paris in May, 1927." (Art Plastics, p. 43)

By the late 1920's Berkander had major competition from both New York and New England. Big producers of phenolic resin novelties such as Catalin and Marblette produced jewelry that was bold, colorful and very different from the more delicate celluloid designs. Much of Catalin and Marblette were made in more chunky designs as a result of the resins molding process.

In the making of jewelry, plastics were cast as rods, tubes, and slabs and then sliced into individual pieces or blanks to be formed and finished by the operator. Each worker completed a piece entirely on his own. Braclets and rings were sawed from tubes and then carved by the individual operator. Floral and geometric designs were numerous yet each piece appears quite individual. The tedious hand finishing operation kept cast plastic jewelry in the higher price brackets through the 1940's.

In 1929, the Depression hit the real jewelry market very hard. Plastic jewelry, however thrived for the next decade. It was reported that "40 to 50 percent of the jewelry sales in stores such as Saks, Bonwit's and Miriam Haskell were plastic." (Art Plastics, p. 41)

During the 1930's and '40's, manufacturers used thin sheets of celluloid plastic to make shaped jewelry forms. Dangles for bracelets and necklaces were cut out as flat shapes, then heated in hot water and curved. Hot needles could etch lines for further decoration, such as veins on leaves or scales and fur on fish and animal shapes. The shapes could also be embossed under pressure with machines specially designed for the job.

The practice of plating entire pieces of plastic was first attempted in 1910. It was, however, a fairly complicated electrolytic method and did not become wide spread until the 1940's. Even then it was very time-consuming and had yet to be perfected. Finally, in the 1950's, new techniques made it possible to plate plastics easily with a shiny metal surface.

In addition to plating, many plastics were set with plastic stones made to resemble precious gems. These pieces were higher priced designs but they also became popular. On the other hand, oversized, toylike pins also were created in the 1940's. Many pieces of jewelry that were in imitation of real objects were made at least at life size, such as cherries. Figural pins of birds, animals, people and sports-related objects were made in large numbers. Chanel designed oversized translucent plastic eyeglasses and buttons both of which were studded with rhinestones. Plastic evening jewelry emerged in the form of larger, solid cuff bracelets set with stones and coupled with a matching belt buckle. The world renowned design house of Hermes experimented with plastic to create a bracelet watch decorated with black enamel and set into colored plastic, and a traveling watch. Cartier used acrylics for buckles on evening bags and other such minor embellishments. Elsa Schiaparelli began to use plastics in making jewelry and various trimmings in the late 1930's. One of her most noteable plastic creations was a vinyl collar inbedded with multi-colored metal insects featuring beetles and dragon flies. She also designed an ice cube necklace of pink crystal plastic cubes and unusual belt clasps, one having a pair of hands with painted fingernails. Pins of similar designs are shown on pages 87 and 114 of this book.

The war efforts of the 1940's included a jewelry collection promoted by Lord and Taylor to benefit Mme. Chiang Kai-shek's war orphans fund. Items such as gilt metal and plastic and replicas of Chinese jewelry were offered. In 1941, another wartime promotion took place in England. Lucky Bracelets were featured and sold for roughly one dollar each. They were made from the acrylic scraps used in the manufacture of bullet proof windscreens for Spitfire and Hurricane fighter planes.

The wartime shortages of all types of luxury goods turned many women toward costume jewelry. Glass from Czechoslovakia, which the costume jewelry industry had heavily depended upon was cut off to American manufacturers. Searching for substitutes for glass, various resins were found to be practical. Acrylics molded as gemstones or carved to resemble rock crystal were used as a substitute jewelry.

Following the war, the tendency in jewelry design was away from formal and geometric styles. "Plastic brooches and ear clips in contrasting tones, shown in colors such as cream and coral, or rose-pink and a deeper red were popular, as were imitation Victorian cameos bearing a woman's head." (Art Plastics, p. 62)

The 1950's brought "Pop-It" beads. Each plastic molded bead had a type of plug end socket construction so it could all be attached to another bead to form bracelets and necklaces of vaying lengths and combinations of colors. The beads varied also in size but not in shape and were soon relegated to the status of toys which were more fun to pop than to wear.

Much brightly colored plastic jewelry was manufactured in the 1960's. Clear Lucite beads and cast bracelets were embellished with rhinestones and metal confetti. The bright colors of this jewelry complemented the fashions designed for the young and fun-loving public. Plastic jewelry designs became more imaginative as they gained popularity.

By the 1970's, plastics were used to produce intricately molded settings and gem-like stones for use in other forms of costume jewelry including imitations of expensive, gem-set designs such as the copy of Jackie Onassas's necklace by Kenneth J. Lane.

The examples shown on the following sections display a wide variety of jewelry styles in plastic materials. Some are imitations of natural plastics and expensive gems, some are original forms, the results of designers experimenting with new materials. They are all beginning to take their places in the history of fashion design.

Amber link bracelet. Amber is soft and easily carved as has been done in this example. (Linda Morgan)

Amber necklaces. Both show variations in translucent qualities. The best quality amber is clear, but some are cloudy and some pieces show "stress marks" giving a crackled appearance. (Linda Morgan)

Natural Plastics

If it is understood that plastics are materials that can be softened, molded or pressed into a desired shape, it is apparent that there are numerous materials in nature which can be termed plastic. Natural plastics have been utilized in various ways by different civilizations.

Amber

Amber is a thermoplastic resin, meaning it can be heated, resoftened and remolded many times. Amber is a fossilized resin derived from trees that grew millions of years ago. The color ranges from a pale warm yellow to almost black.

Amber bead necklaces were popular in the early years of this century. To test for amber, heat a pin and insert it into an inconspicuous place on the article. The pin should go in easily. Professional non-destructive tests are recommended.

In the 1920's and 1930's, amber was widely imitated by less expensive synthetic plastics such as Bakelite and celluloid.

Victorian pin designed as rams head made of tortoiseshell. (Michael Greenberg)

Horn and Tortoiseshell

Horn and tortoiseshell are natural organic substances which have been made into jewelry since early times. Natural horn from animals, particularly Buffaloes, was ground, pressed into molds and heated to become a plastic dough. Boxes, buttons, ornamental pins and hair combs were molded in this way until the 1920's when horn was replaced for the most part by celluloid. Natural horn feels hollow and has a crackled, uneven surface. It smoulders when burned and smells like burned hair.

The shells of Hawkskill turtles were used to make small boxes, hair combs and jewelry particularly in the late nineteenth century. The mottled brown coloring of real tortoiseshell is caused by annual growth patterns.

Tortoiseshell has an irregular natural grain, burns with a flame and gives off an odor like burned hair.

Synthetic plastic imitations of tortoiseshell were among the early efforts of plastic manufacturers.

Gutta Percha

In 1843 Dr. Mongomerie, a Malayan surgeon found Maylay natives using the vegetable material gutta percha, a gum elastic, to make knife handles and other articles. It was a hard material that was scraped by hand from the Palaquium trees in Malaya, Borneo and Sumatra. Gutta percha was first softened in hot water and then pressed by hand into the desired shape.

Dr. Montgomerie's studies provided the impetus for the founding of the Gutta Percha Company in 1845, which remained in business until 1930. It was discovered that gutta percha had excellent electrical properties even when submerged in water and therefore, it soon became a major ocean cable insulation material. For a time, gutta percha was also used to make billiard balls.

Gutta percha jewelry can be found as bracelets, pins and earrings.

Papier-mâché and Wood Pulp

Papier mâché and pulp ware were used primarily for decorative purposes such as trays, tea caddies and card cases which were very popular in the 1830's. One of the first pulp ware manufacturing companies was the Patent Pulp Manufacturing Company which began molding pulp ware in 1879 and continued until 1940.

Papier mâché is created by combining finely ground paper or wood pulp with animal glue or gum arabic and pressing it into a mold with reinforcing wire before drying. A more contemporary process was shaping layers of damp paper over a mold. Papier mâché jewelry was made as earrings, bangle bracelets, and pins. Due to the fragility of the material, few of these examples survive today. Papier mâché feels warm to the touch.

Vulcanite, Hard Rubber

Hard rubber which was the predecessor to vulcanite has been collected from the trees in Brazil for centuries. In 1820 it was discovered by Thomas Hancock that if rubber was cut up, heated and combined with a filler it could be molded into waterproof products. In 1839, as research continued, vulcanization was discovered. Rubber combined with sulfer creates a compound that is moldable and is uneffected by changes in temperature while at the same time, possessing a rubbery, resilent property. This discovery was made by Charles Goodyear who in effect had created the first commercially successful thermoset plastic.

Between 1861 and 1877, England's Queen Victoria permitted only black jewelry to be worn in her presence at court out of respectful mourning for her late husband Albert. This requirement set a fashion precedent which the English-speaking world followed. Black jet is an expensively-produced opal derivative mined in England from which black jewelry was made at this time. Alternatives were soon found in less expensive materials such as pressed horn, celluloid, casein and vulcanite. There are not many remaining examples of vulcanite jewelry but their place among early plastics must be noted.

Bois Durci

Bois Durci was a thermoset molding material patented in 1855 by Lepage in Paris. This compound was a blend of sawdust, blood, egg albumen or geletin that was dried. Once it was compressed and heated, the substance became dark brown or black. Now very rare, Bois Durci moldings were common from 1860 to 1876. Lepage molded jewelry, combs, chess pieces and plaques.

Shellac

Shellac comes from the secretion of the *Croccus lacca* beetle found today in India and Malaya. The Egyptians used shellac to coat their mummies thousands of years ago. When shellac was mixed with fillers, it became a tough and moldable compound.

When shellac is pierced by a hat pin, it yields readily. When burned, shellac gives off a slight smell like sealing wax.

Shellac was first molded in the United States by Samuel Peck in the early 1850's to create "union cases." These became known as dagurreotype cases and were press-molded from a mixture of wood flour bound with shellac which gave the compound the ability to produce very fine detail.

In Feburary of 1862, J. L. Baldwin obtained a U.S. Patent for his method of molding daguerrotype photo cases. His material was even called "plastic", even though its ingredients were of a mysterious concoction. Another patent, entitled "Compound for Picture Frames" called "for a material consisting of straw pulp mixed with one-half ounce of gum shellac, a quantity of alcohol to cut the gum, one-half ounce of glue, one-half pint of molasses, one-half pint of glycerine, and a quantity of ammoniacal solution of copper to make the pulp moist".

Daguerrotype cases were the most popular items produced in this kind of early plastic, but medallions, small boxes, soap containers, sewing kits, mirror backs and combs were also being made from it in the late-19th century.

Two early bracelets in Victorian style, both using gutta percha. Delicate bracelet patented 1884. Bracelet with wide band and jet carved bouquet decoration in relief. (Ann's Arts)

Two distinctly different hair combs. Black hair comb of gutta percha with chain links. Yellow horn comb with cut steel detail. (Patricia Funt)

Double chain of Celluloid oval links with pendant maple leaves of varicolored Celluloid amber tones, c. 1920's. (Smithsonian Institution)

Early example of necklace using gutta percha ornamentation in the form of black open circles surrounded and attached to one another with gilt metal, c. 1900. (Patricia Funt)

Gutta percha bracelets, both with wide bands and cameo style adornment. (Patricia Funt)

Synthetic Plastics

All plastics, no matter what their source, fall into one of two categories depending upon how they respond to heat. A plastic that can be repeatedly softened by heat and re-formed, like wax, is called a *thermoplastic*. This type retains its plastics qualities indefinitely. Natural plastics and cellulosics fall into this group. A plastic that once molded can never be re-softened or returned to a moldable state, like concrete is called a *thermoset*. Bakelite is an example of a thermoset plastic.

Collodian

The Swiss chemist Christian Schoenbine originally developed celluloid nitrate as early as the 1840's by combining wood or cotton fibers with nitric and sulfuric acids. This resulted in a highly flammable doughy material which was then used for explosives, called collodian. It did have, however, moldable properties that were of interest to other inventors.

Parkesene *(Xylonite, Ivoride)*

Alexander Parkes of England experimented with an early form of celluloid nitrate and developed a semi-synthetic plastic in 1855 which he called Parkesene. He had combined cotton fibers, or wood flour, in nitric and sulphuric acids and had plasticized it using oils. Parkesene was eventually patented in 1867.

Parkes failed to make a commercial success of his Parkesene business and sold it to another Englishman Daniel Spill. Spill produced Parkesene in his own factory under the names of Xylonite and Ivoride. However, Spill was no more successful than Parkes had been and from 1865 to 1890 his business suffered continual setbacks.

Examples of Parkesene are cool to the touch, like ceramics.

Celluloid

The invention and practical production of celluloid was the first real synthetic milestone. At the same time that Parkes and Spill were experimenting with Parkesene in England, John Wesley Hyatt was working with a similar compound in Albany, New York. Inspired by the promise of a $10,000 prize for developing an inexpensive material to replace ivory for billiard balls, Hyatt experimented with cellulose nitrate and camphor heated under pressure. When cooled, his mixture became a solid block of clear plastic.

Although he did not receive the prize money he sought, Hyatt patented his material in 1869 and called it "Celluloid". In 1871 he formed The

American Celluloid Company and moved to Newark, New Jersey from where celluloid was marketed throughout the world. By 1880, celluloid was being manufactured in England and France. Eventually, Hyatt's company became the plastic's division of the Celanese Corporation.

Celluloid had wide applications industrially and in the photograpic field. Specifically in jewelry, celluloid was made into hair combs, pins, bracelets and necklaces. It can be colored, made opaque, and etched, and these features all are found in the jewelry examples. Celluloid is extremely flammable and burns with the smell of camphor and nitric acid. It can be corroded by solvents and becomes soft when heated and brittle over time.

In 1920, a method was discovered to use a less-flammable variation of celluloid called cellulose acetate in injection molding processes creating the ability to produce many identical objects at the same time. This discovery helped to popularize plastic jewelry as its cost per item was brought down.

Cellulose acetate is known by several trade names, among them "plastacele" from the E. I. Dupont de Nemours Company of Wilmington, Delaware. A pamphlet published by this company in 1941 illustrates Plastacele jewelry in the forms of a necklace matching the one illustrated on page 17, of this book, bangle bracelets of elasticised links like those on pages 46 and 47, and a pin with dangling cherries like those on pages 75, 80 and 81.

Celluloid and its subsequent forms was made to imitate shell, ivory, coral, bone and hard rubber, tortoiseshell, amber, ebony, onyx and alabaster. It was commonly found in domestic settings as piano keys, napkin rings, camera film, pipe stems, combs, and toys as well as jewelry.

Casein

In 1897 casein plastics were first patented in Germany by W. Kriscke and Adolph Spittler who were looking for a material from which to make white "blackboards." It was manufactured in the United States in 1919. Today it is used primarily as a base for paint and glue. Casein was originally called Galalith from the Greek *gala:* milk and *litho:* stone. In England it was called Erinoid, allegedly because the milk used in the manufacturing process came from Ireland.

Natural casein is a protein found in milk which consists of long polymer molecules. The enzyme rennet taken from the stomach of an unweaned calf, is used to separate the natural casein from skim milk. The curd which settles from this reaction is dried, ground, purified and mixed with appropriate plasticizers and coloring dyes. This combination is then extruded into slots and rods, and hardened in a solution of water and formaldihyde. This new material is casein plastic.

Casein was introduced in Great Britain in 1913 as material for jewelry, knitting needles and crochet hooks.

Similar to celluloid in its visual properties, casein can be made in the same range of colors and patterns. Casein is found commonly as buttons, buckles, hair ornaments, gaming chips, dice, candlesticks and spoons. It can duplicate the natural materials horn, ivory, tortoiseshell and pearl. When heated, casein smells like burned milk or cheese.

Enlargement of salesman's sample showing Bakelite name and trademark. (Smithsonian Institution)

String of graduated oval facet-cut plastic beads of dark amber color, c. 1920's. (Smithsonian Institution)

Salesman's samples of Bakelite colors, c. 1920. (Smithsonian Institution)

Opposite:
Necklace and two medallions in Bakelite. Necklace on brown cord with translucent brown medallion and imbedded design. Round translucent brown medallion. Six sided brown translucent medallion pierced with two holes for hanging. (Smithsonian Institution)

Bakelite

Leo Hendrick Baekeland (1863-1944) was born in Ghent, Belguim, graduated from the University of Ghent in 1882 and entered the United States in 1889. Baekeland lived and worked in Yonkers, New York, where he had a small laboratory near his home.

Educated as a chemist, Baekeland discovered and produced Velox photographic printing paper which he eventually sold to Kodak Company in 1899, at the age of thirty-seven, earning three-quarters of a million dollars. With this fortune as a foundation, he found himself free to pursue independant research.

His reading of scientific journals brought to his attention the work of German chemists who reported a useles, hard material as a result of their work with phenol (carbolic acid) and formaldehyde. Baekeland began studying their experiments and working tirelessly in his laboratory, taking copious notes of all his efforts. Finally, he discovered a workable catalyst for phenol and formaldehyde and was the first person to realize that only under extreme heat and pressure would the resin polymerize as a thermoset.

Baekeland filed his famous patent in the United States on February 18, 1907. This was closely followed by his "Heat and Pressure" patent on July 13, 1907. He called his synthetic resin by the tradename Bakelite and registered the trademark throughout most of the industrial countries.

The substance Baekeland first produced was brittle and a pale amber color. It was not resistant to sun or oxygen and often turned dark. A filler of wood flour, cotton flock, asbestos or mica was added to increase the moldable qualities and add some pigment. These ingredients were combined with the resin and processed, a standard, dependable, uniform product emerged ready for shipment to custom molders.

Baekeland's research, as much as that of any other single individual, provided the foundation for modern polymer science. His studies were very complete and had significance beyond the commercial success of Bakelite. Baekeland's patent was in essence the birth certificate for a whole new industry and his research provided the text on which a whole new branch of science would emerge. Bakelite was not an inferior replacement for a natural material as many synthetics were, or a substitute for materials that were scarce or expensive. "It was superior in chemical, mechanical and physical properties." (J.H. DuBois, report to Plastics History Institute, c. 1950. p. 86, preserved in DuBois Collection, Archives Dept. Smithsonian Inst.)

Bakelite was first used commercially in 1910 and soon replaced amber, hard rubber and cellullid because it was both more economical and a superior substance for many uses. Primarily Bakelite found fame originally as an insulator for all kinds of electical goods, and was used for machine parts that would withstand a great deal of friction.

In 1938, the Bakelite Company became the plastics division of the Union Carbide Company.

Baekeland used lead molds in the ovens with the heat hardenable resins.

In the molds the material was made into stock rods and shapes that lend themselves to being sliced off for bracelets and sold to fabricators. Baekeland maintained a monopoly on the compound until 1926 when the patent expired. Then companies such as Reichold began to produce Bakelite under the name of Catalin which was used to make costume jewelry.

In handling Bakelite it will be found to be warm to the touch, not cold or glassy. The colors were limited to dark shades of brown, red, blue or green. When mixed with other substances the colors can be expanded to include brown and black.

The molded color samples which Bakelite salesmen carried in the late 1920's are shown in the photograph on page 19. Bakelite has been successful in reproducing Jade, Carnelian, and Goldstone.

Bakelite is less than one-half the weight of glass, so the most decorative and large necklace can be worn with comfort. It has a refractive index excelled only by the diamond, and was understandably popular for use in jewelry. Bakelite acquires and retains a high lusterous polish because of its hardness and toughness. It is non-inflammable and has no odor or taste.

About 1925, Bakelite pearls were found to be superior because they not only were indestructable and possess all the best features of other synthetic pearls, they were also light weight, warm to the touch and had a beautiful color and luster to them. They were made of a solid Bakelite base and retain their quality even today.

In the late 1920's Bakelite jewel quality was developed with a wider range of colors available, increased hardness, brilliance and luster which rivaled semi-precious jewels. It was also available in figured, cloudy and

Price list and advertisement for Bakelite bracelets, c. 1924.

Bakelite Bracelets

A FEW popular styles of bracelets, some to match our necklaces, so that the much-in-demand matched sets of necklaces, eardrops and bracelets may be selected.

NO. B9 —A dainty chain mounted bracelet to match necklace B33 (see page 5) and furnished in the same colors .... ea. **$1.50**

NO. BR1—A lustrous circlet for the wrist, Amber, Cloudy Amber, Rose, Apple Green, Ruby, Sapphire, Jet, Violet .... doz. **$7.20**

NO. BR2—As above but larger, an arm bracelet........................ doz. **$8.40**

NO. BF1—Like BR1 but hand faceted in diamond cut .... doz. **$10.80**

NO. BF2—Like BF1 but arm size .... doz. **$13.20**

BEAD BRACELETS to match our round bead necklaces and available in all necklace shades. See page 9. Offered in three bead sizes as follows:

8 m/m .... ea.	**$1.80**
10 m/m .... ea.	**$2.00**
12 m/m .... ea.	**$2.20**

Necklace marked "K & L", probably German with three Bakelite ornaments on chrome links. (Karen Carmichael and Wendy Tyson)

Plastic necklace of aqua and white beads in graduated sizes. Black and tan carved beads also graduated. (M. Klein)

Plastic necklaces with variety of shaped beads. (Karen Carmichael and Wendy Tyson)

Two bakelite necklaces. Long beige, black and red drops on metal link chain. Black plastic links with yellow and black beads. (As Time Goes By)

Yellow amber necklaces. The color of amber will vary widely from a pale yellow and honey to reddish-brown, brown, red and almost black. (Linda Morgan)

shimmery iridescent effects. The new material was also able to maintain its color and structure despite exposure to sun and the aging process.

In 1937 it was estimted by *Modern Plastics* magazine, that 5½ million pounds of cast resin had been produced that year. About 40-45% was used in the manufacture of buttons and 7-9% in the making of costume jewelry. All genuine Bakelite was manufactured with a tag attached which bears the trademark 'Bakelite.' This tag was offered to licensed manufactures to insure the customer the authenticity of the material.

Embed Art Company's statement on Bakelite trademarks, 1924.

E VERY article made of genuine Bakelite must bear in addition to the manufacturer's mark, a tag with the trade-mark "BAKELITE." This tag is furnished only to licensed manufacturers, is found only on articles made from genuine Bakelite materials, and is **your** guarantee and your customer's protection against inferior or infringing merchandise.

Every Embed Art product bears this tag of genuineness.

Look for this tag on all Bakelite Jewelry articles

Acrylic Plastics *(Lucite)*

The original studies on acrylic plastics were done in Germany by Dr. Otto Rohn in 1901. By 1931 acrylics were being manufactured commercially as coating materials and safety bonding for glass. The acrylic plastics have crystal clarity, extreme colorability and valuable optical properties.

Two of the most well known acrylic resins are known today by their trade names Plexiglas and Lucite. They are thermoplastics and are among the most easily worked and polished. Acrylics are able to maintain their stability better than most other plastics.

An acrylic resin can be tinted any color or be used in a clear state. Acrylic jewelry was first designed and produced in Germany in the 1930's. Predominently, these were faceted, engraved, molded and carved pieces like crystals.

It was reported in the May 16, 1941 *New York Times* that the patent for Lucite was given to Maximilian C. Meyer the president of Joseph H. Meyer Bros., a costume jewelry manufacturer in New York City.

The E. I. Dupont Company produced acrylic resins under the name of Lucite during World War II to make bomber nosecone and gun turrets. Lucite has since been made into countless practical items for the home as well as beads and bracelets incorporating colored metallic pieces and rhinestones. Examples of rings, earrings and pins of Lucite appear in the following sections.

Bakelite necklace with brown beads of uniform size. C. 1920. Bakelite was made in round and faceted beads ranging in size from 6½ to 20 mm diameters. (Smithsonian Institution)

Button necklace made from turquoise plastic buttons with a pearl in the center of each. (Jackie Fleischmann)

Plastic butterfly pin. Two plastic necklaces both with plastic chains. (As Time Goes By)

Alternating black beads with variously shaped and colored beads strung on black cord. Possibly Italian in origin, c. 1950. (Linda Morgan)

Plastic necklace in floral motif. Clear, green and white beads are used to design choker. (M. Klein)

Necklaces

Plastic link chain with plastic beads hanging from the links to form pendant style. (Jackie Fleischmann)

Advertisement for Bakelite pearls, 1924.

BAKELITE PEARL CHOKERS

Here are the Bakelite Pearl Chokers now so extremely popular. They need only to be displayed to be quickly. sold. Any woman will prize these lustrous pearls. They are very smart and effective, their dainty beauty having a distinct appeal—an unusual opportunity for increased sales and quick profits. Their superior quality assures lasting pleasure and satisfaction.

No. P-12—The medium or 12 m/m size bead............................Each, $6.00
No. P-125—As above but with alternating seed pearls.......................Each, 6.00
No. P-15—Large or 15 m/m size bead..................................Each, 7.00
No. P-155—As above but alternating seed pearls.........................Each, 7.00

All the above in any of the Bakelite Pearl colors or combinations of any two colors, alternating Pink and Rose or Primrose and Black pearls make particularly attractive combinations.

The clasps on all Bakelite Pearls are of sterling silver filigree, strongly made for durability as well as beauty. Many are set with finely cut stones—and identically fashioned clasps on the various items allow the selection of really "matched" costume sets.

Plastic "grey pearl" necklace strung on white thread. Grey plastic "pearl" bead on yellow metal straight pin. C. 1920's. (Smithsonian Institution)

Bakelite necklaces in popular acorn and oak leaf design. One on clear plastic chain and one with brass chain. (As Time Goes By)

Clear Lucite necklace and earrings by *Castlecliff.* Red strawberry pendant necklace also Lucite. Bakelite jewelry box, c. 1930's. (Karen Carmichael and Wendy Tyson)

Three red necklaces, two with matching plastic chains. Center necklace on metal chain. (As Time Goes By)

Collage of Bakelite necklaces, assorted colors and types of design. Examples of beads in imitation of coral and jet as well as those utilizing the natural beauty of Bakelite itself. (Terry Rogers)

SMOOTH ROUND BEAD UNIFORM NECKLACES

Universally popular, these necklaces have become staple year-in-year-out favorites. The above illustration can only suggest the perfectly shaped lustrous beads, and fails to convey the fire in their clear colors or the soft velvety glow of their translucent effects. Expertly made of perfectly matched beads, strung on finest silk fish-line; all bead sizes from the small 8 m/m to the imposing 18 m/m. All standard lengths from choker to 60" or longer if desired. Rondelles between beads if so ordered, at same price.

Colors—Amber, Jet, Ruby, Jade, Carnelian, Emerald, Sun-Glow, Gold-tone, Amber Flitter, Mourning, Chinese Amber.

LENGTH

Bead Size	Choker	27"	30"	33"	36"	40"	50"	60"
8 m/m	....	$4.30	$4.70	$5.10	$5.60	$6.20	$7.50	$9.00
10 m/m	....	4.40	4.70	5.10	5.50	6.20	7.60	9.10
12 m/m	$2.30	4.00	4.50	4.90	5.30	5.80	7.20	8.50
15 m/m	3.00	5.00	5.50	6.20	6.60	7.40	9.00	10.70
18 m/m	4.30	6.80	7.60	8.20	9.00	9.90	12.50	14.40

To order, specify "Round Smooth Uniform Necklaces" and give length, bead size, color and whether rondelles are wanted. See page 28 for actual bead sizes.

Available also in Bakelite-Jewel Quality at 50% increase over above prices. See pages 15 and 27.

Example of advertisement for beaded necklaces made of Bakelite, 1924.

Reproduction of 1924 advertisement for Bakelite jewelry manufactured by the Embed Art Company.

Contemporary plastic chain necklace, c. 1986. (Karen Carmichael)

Black plastic chain bracelet and necklace by Trifari. (Karen Carmichael)

White plastic and brass link chain supports a bib of similar links with colored wooden beads. (M. Klein)

Plastic pierced drop necklace on plastic chain. Plastic amber colored fish pin. Purple and blue plastic flower pin. Oval backed pin with carved floral design. (Lorraine Matt)

Plastic and wood necklace. Multi-colored plastic chain hlds groups of roughly squared wooden beads enhanced with small plastic beads and fastened with metal links and wire. (Karen Carmichael and Wendy Tyson)

Bakelite bracelet with gold colored chain and dark strawberries and leaves. Bakelite necklace with amber colored fruit and leaves, c. 1930's and 1940's. (Karen Carmichael and Wendy Tyson)

Bakelite necklace with clear link chain and amber and brown square beads. Green Bakelite bracelet with carved flowers and leaves. (Karen Carmichael and Wendy Tyson)

Three Bakelite necklaces and a Bakelite bracelet. Variety of shapes used in design of necklaces exemplify the versatility of bakelite material. (As Time Goes By)

Bakelite necklace on brown cord. (Wendy Tyson)

Bakelite ivory colored beads with gold spacers and graduated pendant. (M. Klein)

Designs in Bakelite and chrome from Germany. Matching light green bracelet and necklace. Chrome used in combination with dark green bakelite to create contemporary look. Bakelite colored to resemble ivory and enhanced with chrome beads and disks. (As Time Goes By)

Three plastic floral groups on silk woven cord to form choker. (M. Klein)

Assortment of Bakelite jewelry, all having the popular acorn and maple leaf theme. (Karen Carmichael and Wendy Tyson)

Celluloid pin and necklace in red leaf form. (Karen Carmichael and Wendy Tyson)

Opposite:
Necklace of black plastic flowers each with rhinestone center. Selected flowers surrounded by rhinestones, c. 1970 by *Kenneth J. Lane.*

Kenneth J. Lane's faux pearl and coral necklace with matching earrings and stick pin. The imitation coral is of plastic, c. 1986.

Bracelets

Translucent gold butterfly bracelet and black with green and gold marbeling Bakelite bracelet. (Angela Kramer, Inc.)

Bakelite belt buckle with gold toned face design. Four Bakelite bangle bracelets. Black bracelet has rhinestones set in as stars. Ivory colored bracelet has face design incised into the plastic. (Muriel Karasik)

Red plastic coiled snake bracelet connected in links. (Linda Morgan)

Three bangle bracelets by *Monet,* "Directives," c. 1980. (Karen Carmichael)

Matching plastic bracelets to be worn above the elbow. Brown and cream tones in exotic design, c. 1930's. (Linda Morgan)

Plastic bangle bracelets. (Karen Carmichael and Wendy Tyson)

Group of carved and decorated bangle bracelets. (As Time Goes By)

Carved Bakelite bracelet, top and side view, c. 1920's.
(Smithsonian Institution)

Ivory colored Bakelite bangles carved with decoration. (M. Klein)

Three hinged Bakelite bracelets with cut work medallions. (Karen Carmichael and Wendy Tyson)

Group of amber toned Bakelite bangle bracelets. (As Time Goes By)

Carved and decorated Bakelite bangles all with hinged openings. (Karen Carmichael and Wendy Tyson)

Layered Bakelite bangle bracelets. (Karen Carmichael and Wendy Tyson)

Chinese carved lacquer bangle bracelet. (Marian C. Carroll)

Plastic bangle bracelets. (Dennis Cogdell)

Varied plastic bangles. (Franny's.)

Trifari hinged bangle bracelet of plastic and chrome, c. 1975.

Two plastic bangle braclets with contrasting color incised into the carved design by Diane von Furstenberg, circa 1980. (Karen Carmichael and Wendy Tyson)

Group of Bakelite bracelets in variety of color, design, and decoration. (Terry Rogers)

Four Bakelite bangle bracelets. (Wendy Tyson)

Group of Bakelite bracelets.
(As Time Goes By)

Group of Bakelite bangle bracelets. (Karen Carmichael and Wendy Tyson)

Polka dot Bakelite bangle bracelets. (Karen Carmichael and Wendy Tyson)

Bakelite bracelets. (As Time Goes By)

Bakelite bracelets. Two linked black bracelets with colored spots. Center yellow bracelet in style of Mah Jong pieces separated by black beads. (Muriel Karasik)

Pair of polka dot bangle bracelets. Black and white bangle decorated with rhinestones. Red linked bracelet (Bizarre Bazaar)

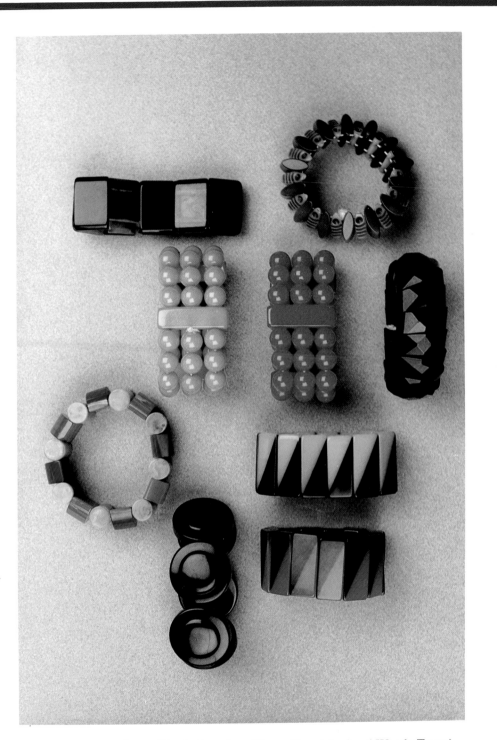

Variety of Bakelite and Lucite bracelets. (Karen Carmichael and Wendy Tyson)

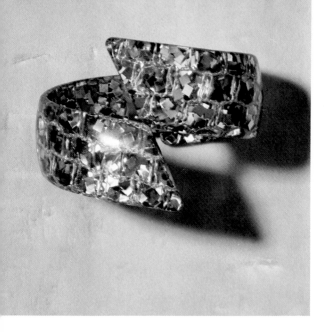

Clear plastic hinged bangle bracelet with glitter inside. (Ann's Arts)

Three unique French plastic bracelets. Multilayered links on elastic. Pastel facet cut links. Diagonal cut layered links, c. 1950. (Linda Morgan)

Red and white beads on elastic cord, form bracelet. Art Deco style European black plastic and chrome expansion bracelet. Four link cuff, signed *Sandra,* in yellow translucent plastic with brass nails. (M. Klein)

Plastic necklace and bracelet with chrome decoration. Butterfly decorated bracelet and geometric hinged bracelet. (Linda Morgan)

Bakelite bracelet of oak leaf and acorn charms on a metal chain. (Wendy Tyson)

Plastic and chrome link bracelet. Each square with an animal figure in chrome, left to right: alligator, frog, bird, elephant, rabbit, cat, monkey and dog. (Muriel Karasik)

Red, black and white Lucite bracelets. 1980's (Karen Carmichael)

Four plastic decorated bangle bracelets. Two pair of earrings in dice style. Five rings with rhinestone decorations. (Karen Carmichael and Wendy Tyson)

Group of Bakelite bangle bracelets, one with matching pair of earrings. (Karen Carmichael and Wendy Tyson)

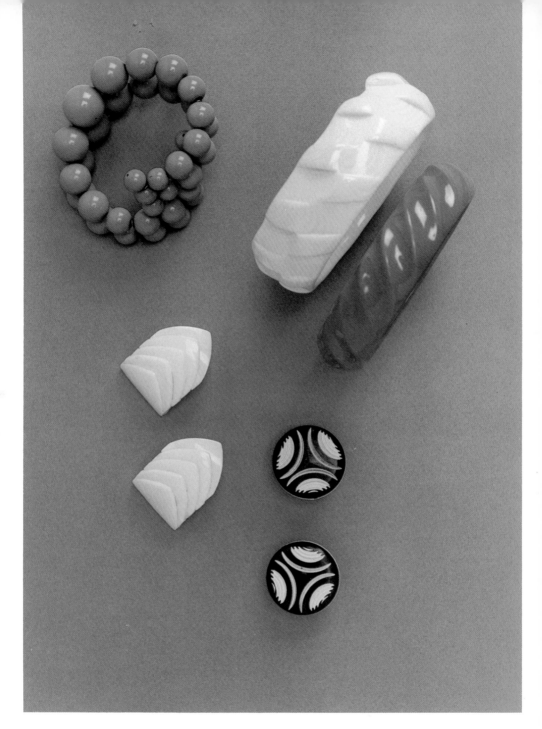

Aqua and ivory colored plastics. Aqua bangle bracelet made in Germany. Ivory look bangle bracelet marked *Napier.* (Karen Carmichael)

Opposite:
Rhinestone decorated bangle bracelets and earrings. Pink and blue stone earrings marked *Weiss.* (Karen Carmichael)

Earrings

Colored plastic flowers on clear plastic coated wire create earrings with tremblant effect. (Jackie Fleischmann)

Plastic earrings by Hobé enhanced with rhinestones and gold colored metal. (Jackie Fleischmann)

Two pair of plastic earrings in floral design complemented by rhinestones. (Jackie Fleischmann)

Three pair of molded plastic earrings show wide flexibility in plastic materials. (Karen Carmichael)

Group of Bakelite earrings in varying designs. (Terry Rogers)

Bakelite earrings in simple geometric patterns and shapes. (Karen Carmichael and Wendy Tyson)

Plastic dangle earrings. (Jackie Fleischmann)

Pair of plastic earrings in image of donkeys carrying packs. Decorated with gilt enamel. (Jackie Fleischmann)

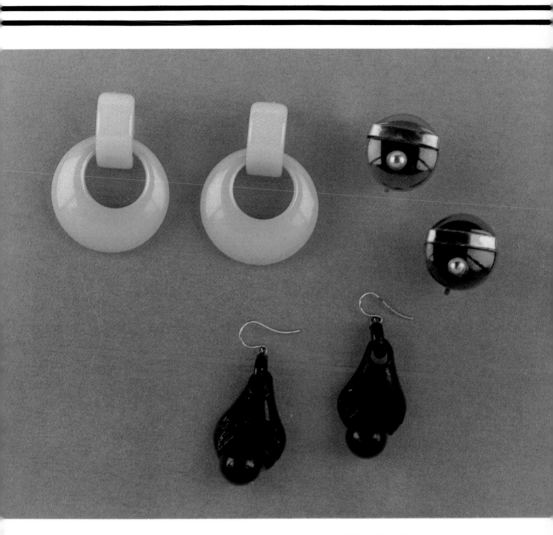

Yellow hoop earrings and black drop earrings are of Bakelite. Green earrings highlighted with metal are plastic. (M. Klein)

Black celluloid and rhinestone dress clips, c. 1920-1930. Celluloid was the first synthetic plastic, patented in 1869. (Dennis Cogdell)

Clock with Westclox movement in round plastic case. Black Bakelite pin with six red and one clear rhinestones on yellow metal background. Red Bakelite pin in leaf shape. (Ann's Arts)

Pins and Clips

Casein and celluloid combined to form two unique dress clips, separated by brass insert, c. 1930. (Dennis Cogdell)

Oval carved Bakelite pin surrounded by metal chain along the edge. (Jackie Fleischmann)

Carved green plastic insert in brass pin setting, c. 1930. (Dennis Cogdell)

Modern plastic cameo applied to Lucite background, c. 1950-1960's. (Dennis Cogdell)

Casein pin with applied Celluloid in cameo style, c. 1930. Casein introduced into jewelry making in 1919 to imitate tortoiseshell, pearl, amber and gold stone. (Dennis Cogdell)

Bakelite pin, set with rhinestones and painted black, c. 1930's. (Dennis Cogdell)

Black molded Bakelite pin with colored raised flower design. (Jackie Fleischmann)

Black glass crescent with beads. Clear Lucite base with etched design and black plastic diamond shape attached. Signed, *Weiss* shamrock pin. (Lorraine Matt)

Black medallion made to imitate black jet cameo. Appears to have hung from black Celluloid chain. (Dennis Cogdell)

Bakelite pin in black with oval drops attached with metal rings. (As Time Goes By)

Transparent amber bar pin with plastic squares connected by metal and plastic links. (As Time Goes By)

Brown Bakelite pin with chrome lollipop decoration. Pair of black Bakelite dress clips also with same chrome lollipop motif. (As Time Goes By)

Laminated Bakelite in the form of three pins of different shapes and large bangle bracelet. (Karen Carmichael and Wendy Tyson)

Amber colored plastic arrow pin with set rhinestones. Ivory colored Bakelite pin with rhinestone studded edge on two sides. (As Time Goes By)

Amber faceted pin of floral design combining opaque and transparent shades of amber. (Linda Morgan)

Yellow and red celluloid flowers with rhinestone enhancement. (Becky Frey)

Bakelite floral motif pin. Multicolored enhanced with set rhinestones, c. 1940. (Dennis Cogdell)

Early style Lucite pin of molded flowers inside clear setting with opaque background. (Dennis Cogdell)

Plastic pins combining color, design, shape and materials. (Linda Morgan)

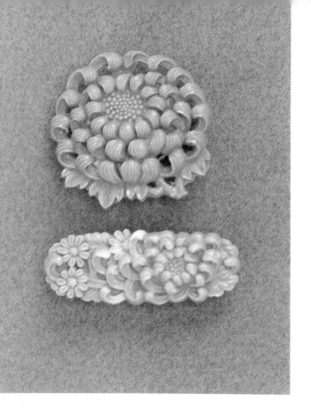

Opposite:
Group of Celluloid pins. Chrysanthemum and basket of flowers pins are marked, Japan. (Mark Solomon)

Two Celluloid pins in imitation of coral. Floral incised decoration. (Karen Carmichael and Wendy Tyson)

Green Bakelite flower with leaves in lighter shade. Brown floral design Bakelite dress clips. Pair of Bakelite earrings in shape of flowers with colored rhinestones. White Bakelite dress clip also in floral motif with dark blue alternating petals and edged leaves. (Terry Rogers)

Assorted styles of Bakelite pins. (As Time Goes By)

Group of Bakelite carved flowers, pins and clips. (Karen Carmichael and Wendy Tyson)

Group of Bakelite pins and two pair of earrings in ever popular floral theme.
(Karen Carmichael and Wendy Tyson)

Opposite:
Bakelite fruit pins. (Karen Carmichael and
Wendy Tyson)

Lucite pins, clear with painted backgrounds. Turtle pin is in wooden frame.
(Wanda Johnson and Karen Carmichael)

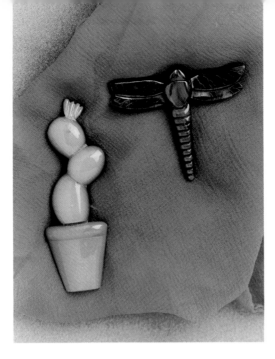

Bakelite cactus plant pin, c. 1930. Green plastic dragonfly pin. (Linda Morgan)

Lucite pin with yellow stems and clear petals tied together with clear Lucite ribbon. Orange plastic leaf clip. Small pin of three plastic limes. Lucite lily with green leaf, orange pistle and white petal. (M. Klein)

Group of Celluloid pins in variety of forms. (Karen Carmichael and Wendy Tyson)

Bakelite pins in forms of potted plant and a palm tree.
(Karen Carmichael and Wendy Tyson)

Two pears together in Bakelite buckle. (Wendy Tyson)

Matching set of necklace and bracelet made in Bakelite. Necklace with red plastic chain and pendant of fruit on brown background. Red links form to make the bracelet with matching medallion attached. (Karen Carmichael and Wendy Tyson)

Popular Bakelite cherries in necklaces, pins and bracelets. All on plastic chains using metal links to attach cherries and leaves. (Karen Carmichael and Wendy Tyson)

Grouping of Bakelite cherry pins in various styles: hearts, bows, bar pins, and leaves. (As Time Goes By)

Red and black Bakelite bows, one with dangling cherries. (Karen Carmichael)

Three Bakelite heart pins, two using cherry motif. (Karen Carmichael)

More Bakelite cherries, pins and earrings c. 1930-1940. (Karen Carmichael and Wendy Tyson)

Assorted designs of Bakelite pins and heart pendant necklace. (Wanda Johnson)

Bakelite pin and earrings in style of hats, c. 1930-1940. (Karen Carmichael and Wendy Tyson)

Pins combining plastic
and Bakelite materials.
(As Time Goes By)

Opposite:
Diverse group of Bakelite pins. (As Time Goes By)

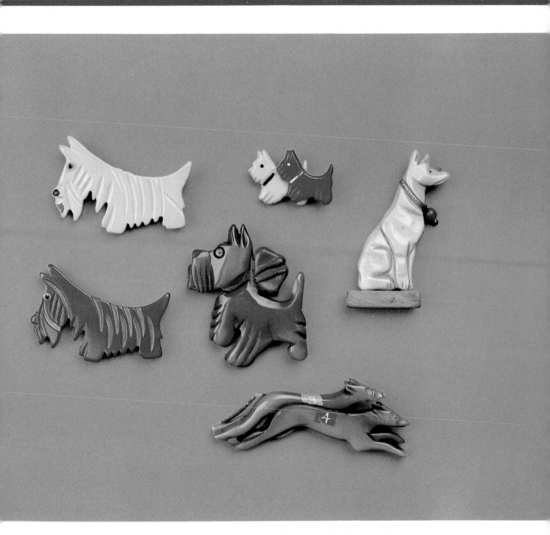

Bakelite dog pins. (Karen Carmichael and Wendy Tyson)

Opposite:
Dog pin with wooden face and Lucite
ears. Two similar Bakelite horse head
pins. Wooden horse head with Lucite
neck and mane. (Terry Rogers)

Opposite:
Plastic Scotty Dog with puppy attached by metal chain. Pair of plastic Scotty Dogs together in a pin. Small plastic dog pin. (Linda Morgan)

Bakelite Scotty Dog pin. Painted collar and tongue, glass eyes, c. 1930. (Dennis Cogdell)

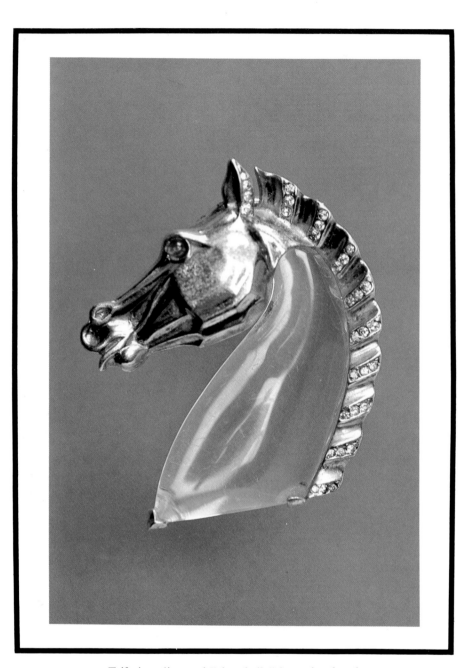

Trifari sterling and "clear belly" horse head and mane with rhinestones and colored glass eye. The name "clear belly" denotes the majority of the body in clear transparent plastic. (Karen Carmichael and Wendy Tyson)

Signed *Trifari* salamander pin in clear belly style.
(Angela Kramer Inc.)

Assorted animal figurals in Bakelite. (As Time Goes By)

Bakelite pins, necklace, earrings and bracelet all in horse motif. (Karen Carmichael and Wendy Tyson)

Exotic animal pins. Turtle pin has green Bakelite shell and clear Lucite body. Giraffe and penguin pins are Bakelite. Bakelite owl pin. Lizard with transparent Bakelite body and sterling legs, head and tail. (Karen Carmichael and Wendy Tyson)

Bakelite pin in shape of parrots. Bakelite money clip with
two red dice attached. (Wendy Tyson)

Plastic bar pin with chrome bands, Art Deco style.
Brown buckle pin in plastic also with chrome decoration.
(M. Klein)

1950's brooch in plastic. Fox design in fuschia with hatched white pattern inside. Pin backing marked *Lea Stein*, Paris. (Linda Morgan)

Parrot head pin combining rhinestones for the head with red Bakelite beak. Possible French origin. (Angela Kramer, Inc.)

Plastic bird pins. (Jackie Fleischmann)

Grouping of plastic bird pins. Red bird with black beak is napkin ring made of Bakelite. (Terry Rogers)

Clear Lucite animals, some with painted details, others with colored Lucite enhancement. (Karen Carmichael and Wendy Tyson)

Examples of Bakelite in pins and earrings, c. 1930-1940. (Karen Carmichael and Wendy Tyson)

Yellow plastic parrot with blue rhinestone eye. Signed *Buch and Deichmann Copenhagen, Denmark.* (Wanda Johnson)

Assorted Lucite pins in animal, bird, fish and insect forms. (Karen Carmichael and Wendy Tyson)

Green plastic frog with yellow metal backing. Peach colored plastic frogs also on yellow metal backing. Green plastic frog on ladder. (Linda Morgan)

Plastic coral with faux pearls on gold filled hinged bracelet, signed *Miriam Haskell.* French fish pin with red and green crystal beads, faux pearls and plastic coral, marked *Dépose.* Plastic coral pin made in Austira. Gold filled wires entwine with light green crystals and dark geen enamel leaves. (Muriel Karasik)

Black Bakelite fish pin. Transparent Lucite fish pin. (Terry Rogers)

Bakelite and Lucite marine life pins, c. 1930-1940. (Karen Carmichael and Wendy Tyson)

Bakelite pins. (Mark Solomon)

Green translucent plastic cicadar, c. 1920-1930. (Bizarre Bazaar)

Three examples of Bakelite hand pins, design made popular by Co Co Chanel.
(Wendy Tyson and Wanda Johnson)

Pins in the forms of people, faces and hands, all made from Bakelite. (Karen Carmichael and Wendy Tyson)

Child's crib toy in Bakelite. Painted eyes and held together on rawhide cord, c. 1930. (Dennis Cogdell)

1950's pin of Bakelite and straw in form of pumpkin character. (Angela Kramer, Inc.)

Assortment of Celluloid pins.
(Mark Solomon)

Plastic pin in shape of Uncle Sam's hat. (M. Klein)

Plastic coffee pot charm. (M. Klein)

Celluloid *Popeye* with enamel colors. Layered plastic oval with female face. (M. Klein)

Plastic football pin using metal chain attached at both ends to suspend plastic boot, megaphone and football helmet. (M. Klein)

Bakelite people pins most using plastic rings to create moveable joints. (As Time Goes By)

Plastic and Bakelite combined in pins and bracelet. (Karen Carmichael and Wendy Tyson)

Layered Bakelite belt buckle and cuff bracelet. Ring with clear plastic setting, adorned with blue bead surrounded by rhinestones. Yellow plastic ring layered with black. Green marbeled ring with yellow flat bead. Large red marbeled plastic ring. (Muriel Karasik)

Rings

Three red fish enclosed within yellow Bakelite ring. Red enamel and metal ring, French. (Angela Kramer, Inc.)

Black square ring layered with white plastic. Green translucent center shows (u of w) underneath on layered band. Red marbled rectangular ring. Yellow and tortoiseshell plastic ring. (M. Klein)

Bakelite rings. (Terry Rogers)

Bakelite rings sculpted and layered. (Karen Carmichael and Wendy Tyson)

Men's celluloid rings made by an inmate at a North Carolina state prison probably fashioned from toothbrushes. (Scott Tyson)

Groups

Plastic set of necklace pendant, pin and earrings, c. 1950. (Dennis Cogdell)

Two butterfly pins with matching earrings. (Terry Rogers)

Lucite pin and earring set, c. 1950. (Dennis Cogdell)

Tinted and clear forms of Lucite jewelry. (Karen Carmichael and Wendy Tyson)

White pop-it beads made into a necklace and matching bracelet. (Matilda D. Knowles II)

Set of pink plastic earrings and pin in chrysanthemum form. (Lorraine Matt)

Bakelite set. Scotty Dog pin in black frame and matching Scotty Dog hinged bracelet. (As Time Goes By)

Black plastic and rhinestones in assorted forms. (Karen Carmichael)

Opposite:
The "Jackie" necklace by *Kenneth J. Lane.* This is a copy of an original very elaborate necklace which was encrusted with emeralds, sapphires and rubys. It was given to Jacqueline Onassis by Aristotle Onassis and was later copied by Lane at her request. Lane was given permission to mass market the copies, some of which were done in plastic replicas of coral, turquoise and ivory. This example uses plastic cabochons, gold plated metal and rhinestones and includes matching earrings.

Rhinestone decorated black plastic, 1980's. (Karen Carmichael)

Layered color in Bakelite pin, clip and pair of earrings. (Karen Carmichael and Wendy Tyson)

Opposite:
Colored beads in various shapes and designs create pins and a bracelet. (Karen Carmichael and Wendy Tyson)

Yellow and black cubed bracelet with matching pin. Both made from Bakelite. (Linda Morgan)

Necklace of large green and yellow marbeled square beads with wound wire spacers. Ring to match. Two green plastic carved rings. (As Time Goes By)

Bakelite polka dot sets. (Karen Carmichael and Wendy Tyson)

Bakelite set with tortoise colored link chain from which hang brown and yellow sculpted drops. (As Time Goes By)

Buckles and Buttons

Brown translucent plastic belt. Two link bracelets with buckle motif, c. 1930. (Linda Morgan)

Opposite:
Green and black Bakelite set with metal trim. Hinged bangle bracelet, earrings and dress clips. (Linda Morgan)

Three Bakelite belt buckles and set of clips. (Karen Carmichael and Wendy Tyson)

Arrangement of bar pins and clips in Bakelite, c. 1930-1940. (Karen Carmichael and Wendy Tyson)

Plastic belt buckle with ten matching buttons. (Jackie Fleischmann)

Belt buckle with nine layers of color and matching clip. (Linda Morgan)

Celluloid belt buckle from late 1920's. Fish form painted gold, red and black. (Smithsonian Institution)

Plastic belt buckle of two elephants tugging a black ring. (Linda Morgan)

Bakelite belt buckle of black brick pattern background with white lizard, c. 1930. (Linda Morgan)

Amber bow shape Bakelite belt buckle. (As Time Goes By)

Brown and yellow Bakelite necklace on light brown plastic link chain. (Wendy Tyson)

Round marbled plastic belt buckle. Black and white belt buckle. Silver colored metal belt buckle and matching pin with cabochon style colored plastic stones. (M. Klein)

Yellow plastic and chrome linked belt buckle. (As Time Goes By)

Plastic belt buckles, two showing plastic mother-of-pearl accents. (M. Klein)

Plastic molded buttons. (Jackie Fleischmann)

Amber colored plastic belt buckles. (M. Klein)

Group of Bakelite belt buckles. (Terry Rogers)

Necklace and earring set of red Bakelite with metal floral carved spacers. Green Bakelite link bracelet. Red and white dangle Bakelite earrings. Red linked bracelet in Bakelite with central floral accent. (Karen Carmichael and Wendy Tyson)

Plastic hair ornaments made in Japan. (Maureen McEvoy)

Amber colored plastic bug pin. Black bracelet with carved floral design and hinged back. Red crescent shaped pin and carved red plastic ring. Spider pin with red plastic body and metal legs. Black plastic sea horse pin. (Bizarre Bazaar)

Matching necklace and earrings with colored confetti suspended in clear Lucite. Lucite wrap bracelet and red Lucite pin. (Karen Carmichael)

Chrome and Bakelite necklaces. German origin. (As Time Goes By)

Bakelite pins and pair of earrings, early examples. (Ann's Arts)

Bakelite and chrome. Bakelite seen here in amber, yellow and purple. (As Time Goes By)

Bibliography

Di Noto, A., *Art Plastics.* New York: Abbeville, 1984.

DuBois, Harry J., "Civil War Plastics". *Plastics World,* June, 1961.

————, and John, Frederick W., *Plastics,* New York: Reinhold Publishing Corporation, 1967.

Field Enterprises, Inc., *The World Book Encyclopedia,* 2, 3, 6, 3, 14 vols. Chicago: Field Enterprises, Inc., 1949.

Katz, Sylvia, *Plastics,* Aylesbury, Bucks: Shire Publications Ltd., 1986.

Lockrey, A.J., *Plastics in the School and Home Workshop,* New York: D. Van Nostrand Company, Inc., 1946.

Plastacele, Dupont Plastics for Products of Today and Tomorrow, 1941.

Revised **Price Guide** © *1994*

Price Guide by Dee Battle, The Old Curiosity Shop, Yalaha, Florida, (904) 324-3023, who is available to answer your questions about plastic jewelry.

Values vary immensely according to an article's condition, location of the market, parts of the country, and overall quality of design. While one must make their own decisions, we can offer a guide.

p-ii. black pin	95-125	p-30. clear link necklace	175-250
face bracelet	special	metal link necklace	250-300
link bracelet	150-225	jewel box	125-175
gold hair ornament	125-175	clear set	150-200
earrings	125-150	strawberry choker	150-200
p-5. pin, gutta percha	125-170	staggered drop necklace	250-325
p-6. trademark	special	round drop necklace	275-350
p-7. pin	175-225	triangle drop necklace	175-300
p-10. heart necklace	150-225	p-31. carved beaded necklace	125-175
pendant necklace	150-200	blue and white necklace	125-175
bracelet	175-250	leaf choker	150-200
p-11. ram pin	250-325	black necklace	225-275
p-14. thin bracelet	175-250	red and black necklace	250-325
thick bracelet	250-325	amber and black necklace	175-225
black comb	250-300	p-33. yellow necklace	75-125
horn comb	225-275	necklace	50-75
necklace	175-225	bracelet	40-60
p-15. necklace	175-250	white necklace	175-225
bracelets	175-250	p-34. white and green pin	75-100
p-18. round pin	75-100	purple pin	95-125
pin, 6-sides	100-125	necklace	125-150
pendant necklace	95-125	fish pin	75-95
bead necklace	150-200	plastic necklace	150-200
p-22. "K & L" necklace	125-175	p-35. dark strawberry	
blue dot necklace	125-175	necklace	175-250
brown dot necklace	175-225	amber fruit necklace	300-375
plastic and metal necklace	75-125	leaf bracelet	95-125
double strand plastic		cube necklace	125-150
necklace	125-175	p-36. orange necklace	195-250
plastic necklace	125-175	brown and orange pendant	
p-23. yellow and black		necklace	275-325
choker	275-350	brown and orange choker	250-300
red and black necklace	325-450	orange bracelet	225-275
amber necklace	150-275	cord necklace	250-300
amber and metal bead		p-37. white pendant necklace	250-300
necklace	150-225	green and chrome necklace	200-250
amber and metal necklace	225-275	green set	450-500
p-25. bead necklace	125-175	white and metal necklace	175-225
p-26. button necklace	195-250	p-38. flower necklace	250-300
butterfly pin	175-225	red bracelet	200-225
green necklace	150-225	green pin	350-400
pink beaded necklace	225-275	brown pin	225-250
p-27. multi color necklace	175-225	black pin	125-150
green and white necklace	125-175	red necklace	225-250
p-29. pearl necklace and pin	150-200	p-39. pin	75-95

necklace	125-150
p-40. set	450-500
p-41. necklace	425-475
p-42. butterfly bracelet	350-425
black bracelet	300-350
black bangle	350-400
taupe bangle	350-400
buckle	250-275
red bangle	400-450
ivory bangle	300-350
p-43. bracelet	225-250
p-44. stripe bangle	50-65
tan bangle	35-45
brown bangle	35-45
p-44. pair bracelets	225-250
p-45. (top) yellow flowered bangle	450-525
amber flowered bangle, if perfect	350-425
yellow and green bangle	550-625
brown and rhinestone bangle	475-525
(bottom) smooth bangle	200-225
carved bangles	225-250
layered bangles	300 up
inlayed bangle	425 up
p-46. brown bangle	250-300
rose carved bangle	125-150
vine carved bangle	50-95
line carved bangle	50-95
crescent carved bangle	75-95
p-47. red bracelet	550 up
black bracelet	250-275
brown bracelet	500 up
assorted carved bangles	95-250
p-48. assorted carved bangles	175-250 each
assorted layered bangles	225-400 each
orange bangle	80-100
p-49. assorted carved bangles (top)	95-125
assorted bangles (bottom)	45-125
p-50. Trifari cuff	125-150
orange incised bangle	95-125
yellow incised bangle	95-125
p-51. (top) bracelets:	
brown	10-20
beige carved	40-60
yellow carved	40-60
white	50-65
orange	95-115
white and brown	75-95
yellow	30-40
(bottom) red bracelet	95-125
ruby with metal stripe bracelet	125-150
Marlowe compact bracelet marked "Parisienne, Reg. U.S. Pat. Off."	250-325

brown and white bracelet	150-175
p-52. (top) carved bangles	95-150
link bracelets	175-225
bracelet with metal chain	135-175
(bottom) carved bracelets	75-150 each
p-53. polka dot bangles	250-500 each
carved bangles	175-300
p-54. black linked bracelets	175-225
mah-jong bracelet	125-150
red bracelet	225-275
pair polka dot bracelets	250-300
black and rhinestone bracelet	175-200
p-55. assorted link bracelets	175-250
p-56. glitter bracelet	125-175
pastel bracelet	150-175
layered bracelet	150-175
stripe bracelet	150-175
p-57. red and white bracelet	75-95
yellow bracelet	150-175
black and chrome bracelet	225-275
green necklace	95-150
layered bracelet	2000 up
peach and chrome bracelet	125-175
butterfly bracelet	250-300
p-58. leaf bracelet	125-175
animal bracelet	175-250
p-59. bracelets	95-125
p-60. bracelets-set of 4	175-225
earrings	50-75 each pair
rings	75-95 each
p-61. green set	95-125
bangles	75-225
p-62. beaded bracelet	30-45
ivory bangle	30-45
aqua bangle	30-45
white earrings	20-25
green earrings	20-25
p-63. sets	225-275
bangles	95-150
earrings	35-45
p-64. floral earrings	95-125
Hobe/* earrings	125-160
p-65. white earrings	25-30
lavender earrings	25-30
p-66. beige earrings	35-55
pink earrings, by Monet, 1980's	35-55
black and red earrings	35-40
p-67. (top) white flower earrings	20-35
yellow earrings	35-40
red flower earrings	40-50
black and tan earrings	45-50
red bead earrings	55-60
(bottom) layered earrings	60-75
red rectangle earrings	30-35
red and yellow layered earrings	75-95

purple marble hoops	45-50
red and white earrings	45-50
red hoops	35-40
black stars	25-30
black loops	60-65
red and chrome metal disc	
earrings	70-90
yellow loops	55-65
p-68. small dangle earrings	45-50
blue dangle earrings	45-50
large dangle earrings	60-70
donkey earrings	35-40
p-69. yellow loops	45-55
green earrings	30-40
black earrings	60-70
p-70. clips	70-80
clock	175-225
black pin	65-70
red pin	40-60
p-71. clips	60-80
p-72. brown pin	75-85
green pin	80-100
p-73. clear cameo	30-45
brown cameo	80-95
p-74. black pin	30-45
floral pin	75-100
p-75. crescent pin	30-45
diamond pin	35-50
shamrock pin	30-45
black medallion, with chain	75-95
p-76. black pin	175-225
cube pin	195-245
black clips	75-100
brown pin	75-100
p-77. layered bangle	950 up
layered pin	295 up
triangle and wedge clips set	125 up
rhinestone arrow pin	125-165
white rhinestone pin	125-165
p-78. amber pin	100-130
pair flower pins	45-75
rhinestone flower pin	175-225
p-79. Lucite pin	30-45
red clip	125-150
yellow clip	135-160
chrome pin	95-125
p-80. (top) round pin	20-30
oval pin	20-30
(bottom) green flower pin	75-95
brown clips	80-95
white and blue earrings	20-25
white clip	20-30
p-81. lace pin	35-40
bird pins	50-60 each
chrysanthemum pin	40-55
flower basket pin	40-55
p-82. (top) crossed feather pin	80-95
rectangle pin	60-70
pineapple pin	175-225

grapes pin	175-225
long feather pin	90-130
flower pin	115-150
banana pin	175-250
palm tree pin	250-300
brown flower pin	75-110
(bottom) leaf pin	175-225
rose pin	65-95
brown clips	125-150 pair
maple leaf pin	45-55
red and beige pin	175-225
brown leaf and flower clips	95-125 pair
brown floral pin	55-75
beige round pin	125-155
p-83. assorted carved pins	225-375
carved earrings	45-65
p-84. pineapple	125-175
cherries	175-225
palm trees side-by-side	150-195
crossed small palm trees	150-195
apple	195-225
turtle	195-225
crossed large palm trees	225-250
orange	225-250
pear	225-250
p-85. fruit pins	175-225 each
dark banana	250 up
light banana	250 up
complete banana bunch	525-600
carrot clip	125-175
green pepper	150-195
oranges, if perfect	325-425
pear, if perfect	275-325
fruit pin	225-300
p-86. cactus	275-325
dragonfly	150-195
clear lilies	150-195
orange carved pin	60-75
lines	75-95
white lily	125-165
p-87. (top) hand	95-125
apple clips	95-125
lemons	95-125
large palm tree	125-150
small palm tree	75-95
bananas	75-95
berries	95-125
bird	75-95
parrot	95-125
pelicans	125-150
crossed palm trees	95-125
insect	75-95
(bottom) potted plant	special
crossed palm trees	350 up
p-88. pears buckle	225-300
p-89. necklace	300-425
bracelet	450 up
p-90. red pin (carved)	250-325
red necklace (carved)	300-400

burgundy pin	300 up
burgundy necklace	450 up
p-91. yellow necklace	450 up
red bracelet (uncarved)	125-175
red necklace (uncarved)	175-225
red pin (uncarved)	125-175
p-92. (top) red leaf	150-195
black bow	275-325
yellow berries	125-145
red heart	300 up
red bar	275-300
red cut log	125-160
(bottom) black	95-125
red bow	150-200
p-93. (top) dark green	225 up
yellow heart	425 up
red heart	275
(bottom) red cut log	125-160
green leaves	150-175
cornucopia	200-250
bowl	250-275
large red cut log	125-160
earrings	50-75
p-94. green bar	125-150
tomato clip	95-125
pineapple button	25-30
dark green flower	75-100
beaded bar	100-125
acorn clips	55-65
star	40-50
crab	175-225
donkey	75-95
heart pin	145-175
heart necklace	60-75
(bottom) hat earrings	60-75
hat pin	300-350
p-95. colored ovals	75-100
palm trees	125-165
berries	225-300
guitar	75-100
safety pin	200-245
sword	140-175
shoes	95-125
p-96. (top) black half moon	
with dangles	225-275
white oval	325 up
dark colored disk bar	250-275
hand	350 up
metal and beads	175-195
layered three section	350 up
bar and bead pin	300-350
white and red disk bar	250-275
layered bracelet	2000 up
(bottom) dog	75-125
horse and boots	250-325
dangling horse	175-225
clear horse	75-125
p-97. yellow Scotty dog	95-110
pair small Scotty dogs	35-75

yellow dog	100-125
brown Scotty dog	125-150
Scotty dog with bow	195-250
racing dogs	300-350
p-98. Scotty dog	125-150
p-99. Scotty dog with puppy	100-125
pair Scotty dogs	85-95
brown dog	100-125
p-100. horse, by Trifari,	
sterling	350 up
p-101. salamander	350 up
p-102. (top) horse	125-150
racing dog	125-150
Scotty dog	100-125
squirrel	90-115
green dog	185-225
spotted dog	125-150
deer	75-95
green pendant pin	125-140
pair horse heads	125-150
(bottom) horse pins	150-375
horse bracelet	125-175
horse necklace and earrings	125-175
horse earrings	75-95
p-103. turtle	175-195
giraffe	250-300
penguin	150-225
owl	150-195
lizard	200-275
p-104. parrot	75-95
dice, money clip	100-125
buckle	75-95
bar pin	75-95
p-105. fox	150 up
p-106. rhinestone parrot	special
pair of flamingos	100-125
red parrot	100-125
p-107. small bird	35-40
pair of birds	75-95
green bird	70-90
USA	75-95
red bird	60-75
p-108. (top) horse	40-85
butterfly	40-85
Scotty dog	95-125
sea horse	85-95
horse head	95-110
horse	95-110
fox	95-110
lobster	100-125
alligator	85-95
(bottom) beige bird	125-175
earrings	95-125
yellow bird	200-250
marlin pin	225-300
bird earrings	50-60
square bird pin	175-225
green bird	125-155
beige bird with green head	175-200

red bird clip	75-95
green bird on perch	175-200
p-109. (top) yellow parrot	55-75
(bottom) ibis	100-125
bird on perch	125-150
flying bird	75-95
giraffe	60-80
red parrot	110-135
rooster	70-90
dragon fly	125-145
marlin, injected	75-100
p-110. (top) green frog	150-175
pair peach frogs	125-145 each
frog on ladder	225-250
(bottom) bracelet	400-450
fish pin	275-300
coral pin	385-425
p-111. (top) clear fish	100-125
black fish	195-250
(bottom) clear fin marlin	250-300
small peach fish	95-125
beige sword fish	125-150
round red fish	250-300
red sword fish	150-175
lobster	325-375
black and white fish	225-275
clear and red fish	125-150
sea shell clip	75-95
green fish	250-300
p-112. brown beetle	90-115
red beetle	115-140
square pin	125-175
ship	95-125
p-113. cicada	175-240
p-114. orange hand	350 up
red hand	400 up
amber hand	225 up
p-115. green and red man	450 up
amber hand	400 up
small hand	200-250
face pin	225-275
man in uniform	450 up
p-116. crib toy	175-250
p-117. pumpkin-head pin	300-350
p-118. elves pin	50-65
cameo	50-65
skater	50-60
roller skates	50-60
hat and cane	55-60
p-119. coffee pot	65-75
top hat	125-150
Popeye	75-85
face	60-70
p-120. football pin	300 up
(bottom) man with bow tie	500 up
man with pink hair	500 up
small blue figure	175-215
cowboy	350-500
figure with red bow	600-750

sailor with yellow legs	600-750
sailor with wooden legs	450-600
p-121. tennis racket	175-225
helmet pin	350 up
bracelet	250-300
p-122. bracelet	750 up
ring with blue stone	95-125
yellow square ring	80-95
yellow round ring	90-100
marbled ring	75-100
buckle	275-300
p-123. red stripe ring	80-90
fish ring	150-200
(bottom) black ring	75-90
green layered ring	150-175
red ring	60-70
yellow and brown ring	40-55
p-124. black carved	40-60
yellow carved	40-60
yellow square	40-60
white rectangle	30-35
blue flower	25-45
black smooth	40-60
p-125. (top) red ring	40-60
yellow irregular shape	40-60
yellow marbled	40-60
yellow and black	40-60
yellow and brown	40-60
(bottom) brown center	90-150
green and yellow	125-150
orange center	150-175
black center	150-175
oval black and white	150-175
square colored center	150-175
p-126. green set	75-125
butterfly set	150-175
p-127. pink set	50-75
square bracelet, hinged	75-95
(bottom) clear bracelets	50-65
colored bracelets	65-75
rings	15-25
earrings	15-25
pin	65-80
p-128. beads, white and	
colors	5-10, a strand
p-129. pink set	60-75
Scotty dog pin	225-275
Scotty dog bracelet	300-350
p-130. heart pin	40-60
bow tie, celluloid	40-60
bracelet, Bakelite	150-200
earrings	40-50
Domino necklace, Bakelite	175-225
p-131. (top) wide solid	
bracelet	45-60
wide link bracelet	75-100
narrow bracelet	50-75
triangle earrings	25-40
disk earrings, Trifari	45-50

heart pin	30-40
necklace	50-60
(bottom) necklace and earrings	1500 up
p-132. earrings	150-200
horizontal clip	275-350
vertical pin	350 up
p-133. cube bracelet & bar	
pin set	450-525
cube dangle pin	325 up
p-134. (top) bracelet and pin	400-450
(bottom) marbled ring	30-45
necklace	125-150
rose cut ring	40-50
line carved ring	50-75
p-135. bracelets, diamonds	600 up, each
earrings	100-150
ring	125-150
polka dot bracelets	175 each
p-136. (top) bracelet	150-175
pin	100-150
necklace	250-300
(bottom) clips	100-125
earrings	60-75
bracelet	350-400
p-137. belt	200-225
narrow bracelet	130-165
wide bracelet	200-250
p-138. (top) tomatoes	150-200
black and white shoe clips	40-50
yellow buckle	75 up
red buckle	150 up
(bottom) green leaf pin	55-75
red pin with carved inset	
beads	125-145
yellow dagger pin	110-135
orange cone pin	95-125
red wing pin	95-125
red with metal accent	90-110
green clips	85-95
orange layered clips	85-95
black dagger pin	85-95
orange spiral pin	125-135
orange diamond pin	65-80
red horse heads pin	125-150
red bar pin	75-95
green and black pin	95-115
p-139. set	125-150
p-140. clip	225-275
buckle	275-350
fish buckle	special

p-141. elephant buckle	250-300
lizard buckle	275-325
p-142. bow shape buckle	125-150
necklace	125-150
p-143. marbled buckle	95-115
black and white buckle	125-145
metal and plastic buckle	
and pin	110-135
p-144. buckle	125-150
p-145. blue buckle	90-95
red buckle	75-85
green buckle	75-95
p-146. button set	65-70
orange and metal buckle	70-85
orange buckle	95-125
p-147. round buckle	45-55
green buckle	55-65
black and white buckle	40-60
p-148. earrings	75-95
necklace and earring set	250-325
green bracelet	100-125
red bracelet	250-300
p-149. hair combs	125-135
bug pin	80-95
black bracelet	175-225
red pin	160-175
red ring	75-90
red spider	40-60
sea horse	175-200
p-150. necklace and earrings	75-100
bracelet	55-75
pin	25-40
p-151. red pendant necklace	175-200
black pendant necklace	95-125
black necklace with three	
beads	100-145
beaded red necklace	140-175
p-152. (top) black with rhine-	
stones pin	50-60
shells and green pin	45-50
sunflower pin	60-75
3 pears pin	65-80
brown shield pin	55-60
red earrings	35-45
beige bow pin	60-75
(bottom) graduated	
crescent necklace	125-150
yellow and chrome beads	200-240
purple and chrome	
necklace	145-175